The Mouse Who Loved the Moon

by Marilee Robin Burton
illustrated by Eva Vagreti Cockrille

MODERN CURRICULUM PRESS
Pearson Learning Group

Manny was a mouse who loved
the moon. He watched it rise every
night. He thought about it every
night.

"I want to go there," Manny told his
best friend, Boris.

Boris loved cheese, not the moon.
"Why?" Boris asked.

"I want to be the first mouse on the moon," said Manny. "I want to go where no mouse has ever gone before."

"How about just eating some cheese?" asked Boris.

"No," said Manny. "I really want to go to the moon. I want to see what is there. I want to be the first mouse to step in moon dust. I want to make paw prints there."

6

"Are you sure you don't just
want some cheese?" Boris asked.

"No," said Manny. "I want to go on a moon walk! I want to look at a moon rock! I want to look at Earth from the moon. I want to go to the moon. I want to see what is there!"

And that is just what Manny did.
He read books. He talked to people.
He studied plans for rockets. And
finally he built his own rocket.

Manny climbed inside. The rocket took off. It circled Earth. It flew through space. It landed on the moon. Then Manny stepped out into the moon dust to see what was there.

Manny looked around. He looked
at Earth. He went to the near side and
the far side. He picked up some rocks.

Then Manny came home.

The rocket splashed down. Boris was waiting for him.

"I missed you," said Boris. "You went where no mouse has ever gone before. What did you see?"

"I finally saw the moon," said
Manny. "I finally saw moon dust.
I finally saw moon rocks."

Early the next morning Manny
went to the store. He got six different
cheeses. Then he went to see Boris.

Manny gave Boris the cheese.
Boris still loved cheese. Manny still
loved the moon. And the two mice
were still best friends.